Tools for
Problem Solving

Level A

STECK-VAUGHN
COMPANY

A Division of Harcourt Brace & Company

Acknowledgments

Executive Editor	Diane Sharpe
Senior Project Editor	Donna Rodgers
Editor	Allison Welch
Design Project Manager	Sheryl Cota
Cover Design	John Harrison
Electronic Production	PC&F, Inc.
Photography	Cover: © Phil Jason/Tony Stone Images;
	p. 1 © Phil Jason/Tony Stone Images; p. 20 (t) © PhotoDisc;
	pp. 20 (m), 22, 23, 24 (both), 26, 27 (ml, mr) Corel;
	pp. 28, 29 (t) © PhotoDisc; p. 29 (b) Corel;
	p. 33 © PhotoDisc; p. 46 (b) © Superstock;
	p.61 © Michael Newman/PhotoEdit;
	Additional photography by Digital Studios.
Illustration	pp. 12–15, 18–21, 23–26, 28, 31, 33, 36, 41–47, 52, 54, 55, 57, 58, 60, 62–64 Dave Blanchette.

Contents

Lesson 1 Write a Plan

Kimberly has 4 .

She has 2 .
How many cows in all?

Write a plan to solve.

Step 1 Write what you need to find out.

How many _____ ?

Step 2 Write what you know.

 _____  _____

Step 3 Tell or draw how you will solve.

Use Objects

Try using objects to count.

How many cows in all?

1. How many ? _____

2. How many ? _____

3. Write a number sentence.
How many cows in all?

_____ + _____ = _____ cows

4. Use objects to tell your own story.
Write the number sentence.

_____ + _____ = _____ cows

Show the cows here.

Practice

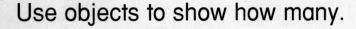

Use objects to show how many.

Quick-Solve 1

Tara has 5 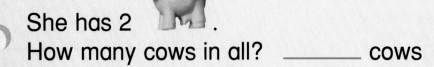 .

She has 2 .
How many cows in all? _____ cows

Quick-Solve 2
The barn has 7 horse stalls.

Tom has 5 .

How many more can he get? _____ horses

Quick-Solve 3

Carlos has 9 .
He has 3 pens.

_____
- - - - - - - - - -
Can he put 4 in each pen? _____

Use What You Know

Use objects to show the animals.

Patty has 3 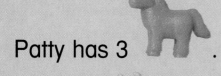.

She has 1 .
How many animals are there in all?

1. How many ? _____

2. How many ? _____

3. Write a number sentence.
   How many animals in all?

   _____ + _____ = _____ animals

4. Use objects to tell your own story.
   Write the number sentence.

   _____ + _____ = _____ animals

Show the animals here.

Lesson 2   Write a Plan

Now try a new problem to find how many in all.

Trevor has 6 pigs.
He has 3 cows.
He has I horse.
How many animals in all?

Write a plan to solve.

Step I Write what you need to find out.

_____

- -

How many _____ ?

Step 2 Write what you know.

_____ pigs   _____ cows   _____ horse

Step 3 Tell or draw how you will solve.

Lesson 3 Use a Picture

Try using a picture to add.

> Some eggs are white.
> Some eggs are brown.
> Some eggs have spots.
> How many eggs in all
> are there?

Look at the picture to find out.

1. How many eggs are white? _____

2. How many eggs are brown? _____

3. How many eggs have spots? _____

Write a number sentence.
How many eggs in all?

___ + ___ + ___ = ___ eggs

Use the picture to tell your own story.
Write the number sentence.

___ + ___ + ___ = ___ ducks

Use Objects

Try using objects to add.

> There are 6 pigs.
> There are 3 cows.
> There is I horse.
> How many animals in all?

1. How many pigs are there? _____

2. How many cows are there? _____

3. How many horses are there? _____

4. Write a number sentence.
   How many animals in all?

___ + ___ + ___ = ___ animals

5. Use objects to tell your own story.
   Write the number sentence.

___ + ___ + ___ = ___ animals

Show the animals here.

Practice

Use objects to add.

Quick-Solve I
Emily has 4 red sheep.
She has 2 yellow sheep.
She has I orange sheep.

How many sheep are there in all?   _____ sheep

Quick-Solve 2
Mike has 3 purple cows.
He has the same number of red cows.
He has the same number of blue cows.

How many cows in all?   _____ cows

Quick Solve 3
Lin has 2 red rabbits.
She has 2 green rabbits.
She has 5 rabbits in all.

How many rabbits are not red or green?   _____ rabbit

Use What You Know

Use objects to add.

Adam has 4 ducks.
He has 4 pigs.
He has 0 horses.
How many animals are
there in all?

I. How many ducks are there? _____

2. How many pigs are there? _____

3. How many horses are there? _____

Show the animal

4. Write a number sentence.
How many animals in all?

___ + ___ + ___ = ___ animals

5. Use objects to tell your own story.
Write the number sentence.

2

3.

4.

5.

___ + ___ + ___ = ___ animals

Practice

Use the picture to solve.

Quick-Solve I
How many horses in all are there?

_____ + _____ + _____ = _____

Quick-Solve 2
How many pigs in all are there?

_____ + _____ + _____ = _____

Quick-Solve 3
How many animals have spots?

_____ + _____ + _____ = _____

Use What You Know

Use the picture to solve.

> Some pigs are sleeping.
> Some pigs are eating.
> Some pigs are in the mud.
> How many pigs in all
> are there?

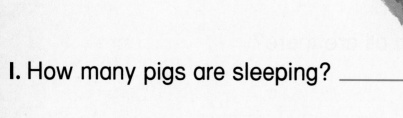

1. How many pigs are sleeping? _____

2. How many pigs are eating? _____

3. How many pigs are in the mud? _____

4. Write a number sentence.
   How many pigs in all are there?

   _____ + _____ + _____ = _____ pigs

5. Write your own number sentence.
   Add any two groups of pigs.

   _____ + _____ = _____ pigs

Using a Picture: Addition of Three Addends

Lesson 4   Solve It Your Way

Choose how you will solve.

> **Use objects or use the picture.**

1. There are 4 cows in the pen.
There are 2 cows on the hill.
There are 4 cows in the barn.
How many cows are there in all?   _____ cows

2. There are 5 horses in the pen.
There is 1 horse on the hill.
There are 4 horses in the barn.
How many horses are there in all?   _____ horses

3. How many animals
are not in the barn?   _____ animals

4. Sam has 4 pigs.
He wants to have 6 pigs.
How many more pigs does he need?   _____ pigs

Practice

Write your own problems.
Use objects or draw pictures.

```
⌐) Quick-Solve I
      There are 6 animals in all.


⌐) _____ + _____ = 6
```

```
⌐) Quick-Solve 2
      There are 10 animals in all.


⌐) _____ + _____ = 10
```

```
⌐) Quick-Solve 3
      There are 9 animals in all.


⌐) _____ + _____ + _____ = 9
```

Applying Strategies

Review   Show What You Know

You have 8 animals.
Some are horses.
Some are pigs.
How many different ways
can you have 8 animals?

1. Write each way.

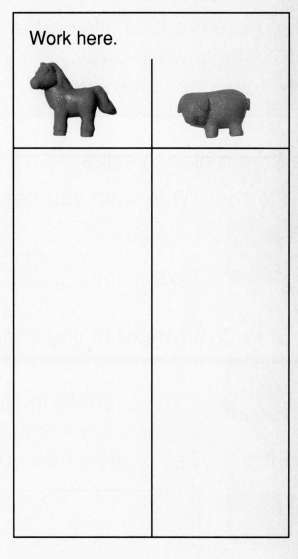

Work here.

_____ + _____ = 8 animals

_____ + _____ = 8 animals

_____ + _____ = 8 animals

_____ + _____ = 8 animals

_____ + _____ = 8 animals

_____ + _____ = 8 animals

_____ + _____ = 8 animals

2. Can you have 3 horses and 6 pigs?
Tell why or why not.

_ _ _ _ _ _ _ _ _ _

_____

_____

3. Can you have 0 horses and 8 pigs?
Tell why or why not.

_ _ _ _ _ _ _ _ _ _

_____

UNIT 2 At the Ocean

Lesson 1 Write a Plan

There are 10 shells on the beach.
3 shells wash away.
How many shells are left?

Write a plan to solve.

Step 1 Write what you need to find out.

_____

- -

How many _____ ?

Step 2 Write what you know.

_____ shells in all   _____ shells wash away

Step 3 Tell or draw how you will solve.

Act It Out

Act out the story.

How many shells are left?

1. Show how many shells are on the beach.

   Write the number. _____ shells in all

2. Make 3 shells wash away.

3. Write how many shells are left. _____ shells

4. Write the number sentence that shows
   how many are left.

   _____ – _____ = _____ shells

Practice

Act out the stories to find how many.

Quick-Solve 1

There are 9 fish.

6 fish swim away.

How many fish are left? _____ fish

Quick-Solve 2

There are 8 turtles.

4 turtles are on the beach.

Some are in the water.

How many turtles are in the water? _____ turtles

Quick-Solve 3

5 shells are on the beach.

2 shells are in the water.

How many more shells are on the beach? _____ shells

Applying Strategies

Use What You Know

Be sure to start with 7 shells.

Act out the story to find how many.

> 7 shells are on the beach.
> Each day I shell washes away.
> How many shells are left each day?

I. Show shells for each day.
Write the number sentence.

Sunday   ____7____ − _____ = _____ shells left

Monday   _____ − _____ = _____ shells left

Tuesday   _____ − _____ = _____ shells left

Wednesday   _____ − _____ = _____ shells left

Thursday   _____ − _____ = _____ shells left

Friday   _____ − _____ = _____ shells left

Saturday   _____ − _____ = _____ shells left

2. After how many days were there no shells left?

_____ days

3. There are 10 fish. 5 fish swim away.
Can there be 6 fish left?

Lesson 2   Write a Plan

Ann sees 6 crabs on a rock.
3 crabs fall in the water.
How many crabs are left on the rock?

Write a plan to solve.

Step 1   Write what you need to find out.

_____

_ _ _ _ _ _ _ _ _ _ _ _ _ _ _ _ _ _

How many _____ ?

Step 2   Write what you know.

_____ crabs in all   _____ crabs fall in

Step 3   Tell or draw how you will solve.

Act It Out

Act out the story to subtract.

How many crabs are left?

I. Show how many crabs are on the rock.

Write the number. _____ crabs in all

2. Make 3 crabs fall in.

3. Write how many crabs are left. _____ crabs

4. Write the number sentence that shows how many are left.

_____ – _____ = _____ crabs

Practice

Act out the stories to find how many.

Quick-Solve I
There are 8 fish.
4 fish swim away.
How many fish are left? _____ fish

Quick-Solve 2
There are 5 turtles.
3 turtles are on the beach.
Some turtles are in the water.
How many turtles are in the water? _____ turtles

Quick-Solve 3
7 crabs are on the beach.
2 crabs are in the water.
How many more crabs are on the beach? _____ crabs

Applying Strategies

Use What You Know

Act out the story to subtract.

> Jane has 10 shells.
> She gives 2 shells to Ann.
> Then she gives 4 shells to Dave.
> How many shells does Jane have left?

Do you have 10 shells?

I. Show the shells Jane has.

Write the number. _____ shells

2. Take away the shells Jane gave to Ann.
Write the number sentence.

_____ – _____ = _____ shells

3. Take away the shells Jane gave to Dave.
Write the number sentence.

_____ – _____ = _____ shells

4. How many shells does Jane have left? _____ shells

5. Now who has the same number of shells

_____

as Jane? _____

Lesson 3 Draw a Picture

Draw a picture to subtract.

> 8 fish are swimming.
> 4 fish swim into a cave.
> 2 fish swim behind a rock.
> How many fish are left?

1. Draw a picture to show the fish in the story.

2. Write the number of fish that are left. _____ fish

3. Draw a picture of your own fish story.

4. Write the number of fish that are left. _____ fish

Drawing a Picture: Subtraction to 10

Practice

Draw a picture to find how many.

Quick-Solve 1

9 shells are on the beach.
Tony picks up 2 shells.
Jane picks up 4 shells.
How many shells are left? _____ shells

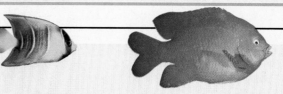

Quick-Solve 2

There are 7 big fish.
There are 10 little fish.
4 little fish swim away.
Are there more little fish or big fish left?

more _____ fish

Quick-Solve 3

9 shells are on the beach.
4 are brown shells.
How many are **not** brown shells? _____ shells

Use What You Know

Draw a picture to find how many.

> 10 crabs are on the beach.
> 4 crabs swim in the water.
> 4 crabs crawl on a rock.
> How many crabs are left on the beach?

1. Draw a picture to show the crabs.

2. Write the number of crabs left on the beach. _____ crabs

3. Draw a new picture. Share it with a friend. Tell a story about your picture.

Lesson 4   Solve It Your Way

Now you get to do it your way.

Choose how you will solve.

Act it Out
Draw a Picture

1. 6 snails are on the beach.
   I snail climbs on a rock.
   3 more snails climb on a rock.
   How many snails are left on the beach?   _____ snails

2. Tammy sees 4 fish.
   All the fish swim behind a rock.
   How many fish can Tammy see now?   _____ fish

3. 5 snails are on the beach.
   8 snails are on the rock.
   4 snails crawl off the rock.
   Are there more snails on the rock or on the beach?

   _____

   on the _____

4. 6 turtles are sleeping on the sand.
   7 turtles are on the rock.
   I turtle falls off the rock into the sea.
   Are more turtles on the sand or on the rock?

   _____

   _____

Practice

Write your own problems.
Act them out or draw pictures.

Quick-Solve I

_____ − _____ = 4 turtles

Quick-Solve 2

_____ − _____ = 2 turtles

Quick-Solve 3

_____ − _____ = 5 turtles

Review   Show What You Know

Work with a partner.
Act out the story or draw a picture.

1. You and a friend are setting up a fish tank.
   You buy some fish.
   You buy 4 striped fish, 1 spotted fish, and 5 plain fish.
   How many fish do you buy?

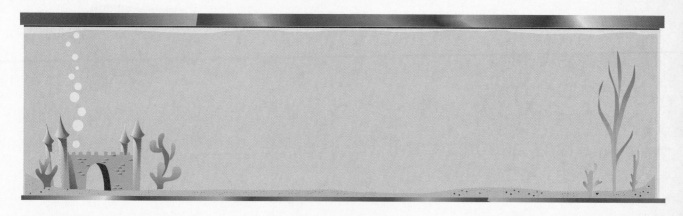

Write a number sentence.

_____ + _____ + _____ = _____ fish

2. There are too many fish in the tank.
   You get another tank.
   You put the same number of fish in each tank.
   How many fish do you put in each tank?   _____ fish

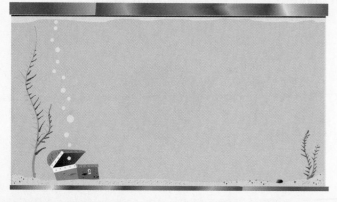

Choose how you will solve.

Now you get to choose.

Use Objects Use a Picture
Act It Out Draw a Picture

1. Sue has 4 pigs.
   She has 2 cows.
   She has 3 horses.
   How many animals are there in all? _____ animals

2. 3 cows are eating.
   3 cows are walking.
   2 cows are sleeping.
   How many cows are there in all? _____ cows

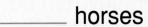

3. 10 horses are brown.
   3 horses are white.
   How many more horses are brown? _____ horses

4. There are 8 shells in a pail.
   3 fall out.
   How many are left? _____ shells

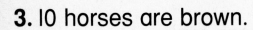

5. You buy 4 white eggs, 1 spotted egg, and
5 brown eggs.
How many eggs do you buy?
Write a number sentence.

_____ + _____ + _____ = _____ eggs

6. How many fish are green?   _____

How many fish are brown?   _____

How many fish have spots?   _____
How many fish in all?
Write a number sentence.

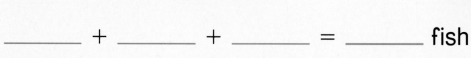

_____ + _____ + _____ = _____ fish

7. Mia has 4 crabs.
She wants to have 9 crabs.
How many more crabs does she need?   _____ crabs

8. You have 9 shells and 3 pails.
You put 2 shells in the first pail.
You put 4 shells in the second pail.
How many shells will be in the third pail?   _____ shells

Patterns Around Me

Lesson 1   Write a Plan

| Color the next three cubes. |

Write a plan to solve.

Step 1   Write what you need to find out.

_____

- -

_____

Step 2   Write what you know.

_____

- -

_____

Step 3   Tell or draw how you will solve.

Draw a Picture

Draw a picture to show the pattern.

Color the next three cubes.

1. There are _____ red cubes in the pattern.

2. There are _____ blue cubes in the pattern.

3. There are _____ yellow cubes in the pattern.

4. What color cube comes first? ☐

5. What color cube comes next? ☐

6. Do you see the pattern?
   Color the three missing cubes.

Practice

Draw a picture to show the pattern.

Quick-Solve 1
Draw what comes next.

Quick-Solve 2
Draw what comes next.

Quick-Solve 3
Draw what comes next.

Use What You Know

Draw a picture to show each pattern.

You may also use objects to make the pattern.

Use triangles and circles. What comes next?

1. Draw the next shapes in the pattern.

2. There are _____ triangles in the pattern.

3. There are _____ circles in the pattern.

4. Draw the next shapes in the pattern.

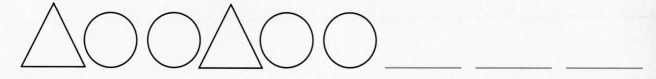

Lesson 2 Write a Plan

You have 3 red squares.
You have 3 blue squares.
How can you make a pattern?

Write a plan to solve.

Step 1 Write what you need to find out.

_____

- -

_____

Step 2 Write what you know.

- -

_____

Step 3 Tell or draw how you will solve.

Writing a Plan: Patterns

Draw a Picture

Draw a picture to make a pattern.

How can you make a pattern?

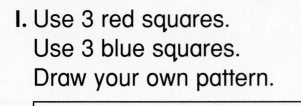

You have 6 squares in all.

1. Use 3 red squares.
   Use 3 blue squares.
   Draw your own pattern.

2. What color did you use first? _____

3. What color did you use next? _____

4. Now draw your own pattern with 7 red and blue squares in all.

5. Does your pattern have more red or blue squares?

   more _____ squares

Practice

Draw pictures to make your own pattern.

Quick-Solve I
Use I blue circle and I yellow square.
Then draw the pattern 2 more times.

There are _____ yellow squares in my pattern.

Quick-Solve 2
Use I red circle and 3 blue triangles.
Then draw the pattern I more time.

There are _____ blue triangles in my pattern.

Quick-Solve 3
Use 2 yellow triangles and 2 red squares.
Then draw the pattern I more time.

There are _____ red squares in my pattern.

Applying Strategies

Use What You Know

Make a pattern for a belt.

I. Draw a pattern on the belt.
Use all the circles and triangles.

Make a pattern for a flag.

2. Draw a pattern on the flag.
Use all the stars, moons, and suns.

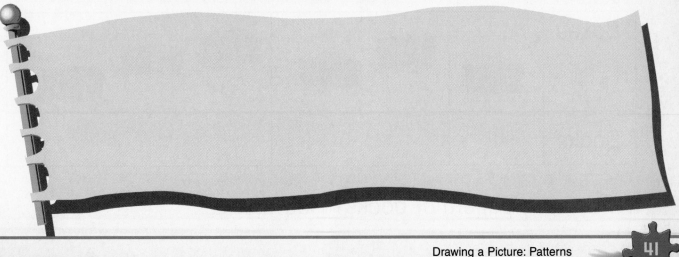

Lesson 3 Make a Table

Make a table to find a number pattern.

> There are 3 bears.
> Each bear has 2 ears.
> How many ears are there in all?

I. Make a table to show the pattern.

Bears			
Ears	2		

What is the pattern of ears? Add _____.

> There are 3 boxes.
> Each box has 4 books.
> How many books are there in all?

2. Make a table to show the pattern.

Boxes			
Books	4		

What is the pattern of books? Add _____.

Making a Table: Patterns

Practice

Make a table to solve.

Quick-Solve 1

There are 3 houses. Each has 3 windows.

Houses			
Windows	3		

What is the pattern of windows? Add _____.

Quick-Solve 2

There are 3 pails. Each has 4 shells.

Pails			
Shells			

What is the pattern of shells? Add _____.

Quick-Solve 3

There are 3 boxes. Each has 5 crayons.

Boxes			
Crayons			

What is the pattern of crayons? Add _____.

Use What You Know

Make a table to solve.

> There are 3 babies.
> How many legs in all?

1. Make a table to show the pattern.

Babies			
Legs	2		

What is the pattern? Add _____.

2. There are 3 bugs.
How many legs in all?

Bugs			
Legs			

What is the pattern? Add _____.

3. There are 3 spiders.
How many legs in all?

Spiders			
Legs			

What is the pattern? Add _____.

Making a Table: Patterns

Lesson 4 Solve It Your Way

Choose how you will solve.

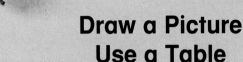

Draw a Picture
Use a Table

Now you get to choose.

1. How many windows are on the houses?

Houses	1	2	3
Windows			

What is the pattern of windows? Add _____.

2. How many petals are on the flowers?

Flowers	1	2	3
Petals			

What is the pattern of petals? Add _____.

3. You have 2 squares and 1 triangle.
   Make a pattern.
   Draw it 3 times.

Practice

Draw a picture or make a table.

Quick-Solve I
Your belt has a pattern.
It has the same number of
circles and triangles.

Quick-Solve 2
Make a pattern using blocks.
There are 3 rectangles, 3
circles, and 3 triangles.

Quick-Solve 3
You have 4 toy horses.
How many legs?

Applying Strategies

Review Show What You Know

1. Draw what comes next.

 _____ _____

2. Draw what comes next.

 _____ _____

3. Each tree has 6 apples.
Show the number pattern.

Trees						
Apples						

4. Each duck has 2 feet.
Show the number pattern.

Ducks						
Feet						

School Fair

Lesson 1 Write a Plan

Kendra has 10¢ to spend at the School Fair. What coins can she have?

Write a plan to solve.

Step 1 Write what you need to find out.

_____

- -

_____

Step 2 Write what you know.

- -

_____

Step 3 Tell or draw how you will solve.

Use Objects

Draw a picture
for each way.

Try using coins.

What coins can Kendra have?

I. Show four ways to make 10¢.
Then draw the coins you used.

2. What are the fewest coins to make 10¢?

_____

- -

_____

3. What are the most coins to make 10¢?

_____

- -

_____

Practice

Use coins to solve.
Then draw a picture.

Quick-Solve 1
Sergio has 15¢.
What coins can he have?

15¢

Quick-Solve 2
Lisa has 18¢.
What coins can she have?

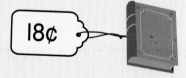

18¢

Quick-Solve 3
An eraser costs 22¢.
What coins can Maki use to
pay for the eraser?

22¢

Use What You Know

Use dimes, nickels, and pennies.
Draw a picture.

> Show three ways to make 25¢.

1. Draw the coins.

2. What are the fewest coins to make 25¢?

_____

- -

_____

3. What are the most coins to make 25¢?

_____

- -

_____

4. Write an amount between 12¢ and 23¢. _____
Ask a friend to show the amount 3 ways.

Lesson 2   Write a Plan

You have 18¢.
What can you buy?
Show the coins you need
to buy it.

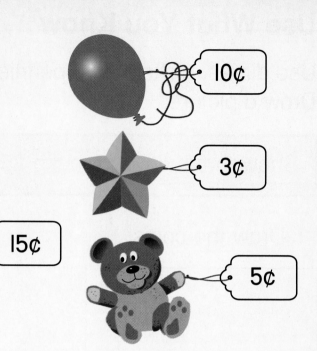

10¢

3¢

15¢

5¢

Write a plan to solve.

Step 1   Write what you need to find out.

_____

- - - - - - - - - - - - - - - - - -

_____

Step 2   Write what you know.

_____

- - - - - - - - - - - - - - - - - -

_____

Step 3   Tell or draw how you will solve.

Writing a Plan: Money

Use Objects

Look at the picture on page 52.

Use objects. Then draw a picture to solve.

You have 18¢.
Show what you can buy.
Show the coins you need to buy it.

I. Draw what you can buy.	Draw the coins you need.

2. Draw what you can buy.	Draw the coins you need.

3. Can you buy the balloon and the book? _____

Practice

Use coins to solve.
Then draw a picture.

Quick-Solve 1
Cara wants a hat.
What coins can she use to pay for it?

Quick-Solve 2
Brian wants cotton candy and a book.
What coins can he use to pay for them?

Quick-Solve 3
Dan has 15¢.
Can he buy cotton candy and a toy elephant?

Use What You Know

Use objects to solve.
Then draw a picture.

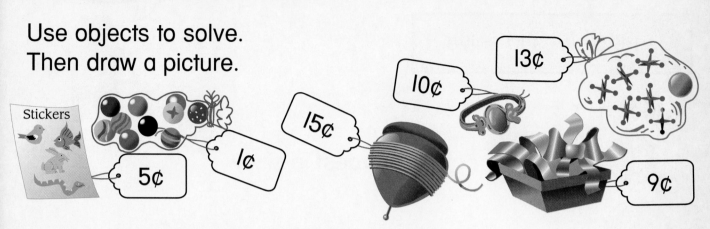

I. You can spend 16¢ at the fair.

Draw what you can buy.	Draw the coins you can use.

2. What can you buy for I dime and 3 pennies?

_____

- -

_____

_____

3. Jane has 20¢.
Can she buy a top and some stickers? _____

Lesson 3 Use Logic

Use coins.

Use the clues to solve.

1. Match.

I am the largest in size.

I am the largest amount.

I am a different color.

2. You can trade me for 10 pennies.

_____

- -

What am I? _____

3. I have 3 coins in my pocket.
They equal 15¢.
Draw my coins.

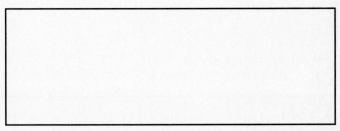

4. Which group of coins is not the same amount?

Practice

Use the clues to solve.

Quick-Solve I
Would you like 10 pennies
or 2 dimes to spend at the
School Fair? Why?

Quick-Solve 2
Sam has 3 coins.
They equal 12¢.
What are the coins?

Quick-Solve 3
Mara used 5 coins.
What did she buy?

16¢   13¢

20¢

Use What You Know

Use logic to solve.
Circle **yes** or **no**.

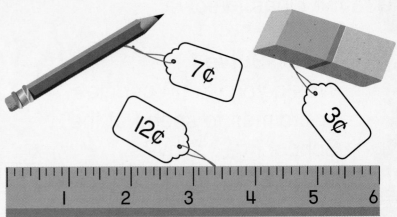

I. You have 20¢.

Can you buy the ruler and the book?   yes   no

Can you buy the book and the pencil?   yes   no

2. You have I nickel and 8 pennies.

Can you buy the ruler?   yes   no

Can you buy the pencil and the eraser?   yes   no

3. You have I dime and 6 pennies.

Can you buy the pen and the eraser?   yes   no

Can you buy the pencil and the ruler?   yes   no

4. Look at all the items.

Does the book cost more than 3 nickels?   yes   no

Does the pen cost more than I dime?   yes   no

Lesson 4　Solve It Your Way

Choose how you will solve.

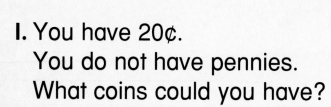

**Use Objects
Use Logic**

Now you get
to choose.

I. You have 20¢.
You do not have pennies.
What coins could you have?

2. Are 2 dimes the same as 4 nickels? _____

3. Kitty has 14 nickels.
Ruth has 2 dimes.
Who has more money?

4. Tom has 4 nickels.
Su has 13 pennies.
Who has more money?

Practice

Use objects or use logic.

Quick-Solve 1
You have 25¢.
You do not have pennies.
Show what coins you can have.

Quick-Solve 2
A toy bear costs 17¢.
You have nickels and pennies.
Show how you can pay.

Quick-Solve 3
Are 2 dimes the same as
5 nickels?
Show how you know.

Show What You Know • • • • • • • • • • • • •

Now work with a partner.
Solve each problem.

1. You have 23¢.
Some coins are dimes.
Some are nickels.
Some are pennies.
What coins can you have?

_____

2. You have 23¢.
Can you have I dime and 8 pennies?
Show why or why not.

_____

3. You have 23¢.
Can you have 4 nickels and 5 pennies?
Show why or why not.

4. Tara has one coin.
It is equal to two nickels.
What coin does Tara have?

Now you get to choose.

Choose how you will solve.

Draw a Picture   **Use Objects**
Make a Table   **Use Logic**

1. What two shapes come next?

_____ _____

2. What coins are missing?

_____ _____ _____

3. How many ears?
Complete the table.

Clowns						
Ears						

What is the pattern of ears? Add _____.

4. A bracelet costs 13¢.
What coins can you use to buy it?

5. What are the fewest coins that make 13¢?

_____

- -

_____

6. Mark has 5 coins in his pocket.
They equal 17¢.
Draw Mark's coins.

7. You have 2 dimes.
What can you buy?

_____

- - - - - - - - - - - - - - - - - -

_____

- - - - - - - - - - - - - - - - - -

_____

Final Review

Wow! You can choose from all these!

Read each problem.
Choose how you will solve.

Use Objects	Use a Picture
Act It Out	Draw a Picture
Use Logic	Make a Table

1. There are 9 shells in the water.
   There are 2 shells in the pail.
   How many more shells are in the water? _____ shells

2. How many shells are white?
   How many shells are brown?
   How many shells are spotted?
   How many shells in all?

   _____ + _____ + _____ = _____ shells

3. How many petals are on the flowers?

Flowers	🌼	🌼 🌼	🌼 🌼 🌼
Petals	5		

   What is the pattern of petals? Add _____.

4. Are 2 dimes and I nickel the same as _____
   3 nickels and 10 pennies?   - - - - - - - - - - - - - - - - -
   Tell how you know.   _____

64

Cumulative Review: Applying Strategies